Database
and
Physical Process Design

London: The Stationery Office

Central Computer and Telecommunications Agency

Published with the permission of the Central Computer and Telecommunications Agency on behalf of the Controller of Her Majesty's Stationery Office.

© Crown Copyright 2000

First published 2000

ISBN 0 11 330876 0

Titles within the Business Systems Development series include:

SSADM Foundation	ISBN 0 11 330870 1
Data Modelling	ISBN 0 11 330871 X
The Business Context	ISBN 0 11 330872 8
User-Centred Design	ISBN 0 11 330873 6
Behaviour and Process Modelling	ISBN 0 11 330874 4
Function Modelling	ISBN 0 11 330875 2
Database and Physical Process Design	ISBN 0 11 330876 0
Also available as a boxed set	ISBN 0 11 330883 3

For further information on CCTA products
Contact:

CCTA Help Desk
Rosebery Court
St Andrews Business Park
Norwich NR7 0HS
Tel 01603 704567 GTN 3040 4567

CONTENTS

FORWARD

The Business Systems Development (BSD) series represents 'best practice' approaches to investigating, modelling and specifying Information Systems. The techniques described within this series have been used on systems development projects for a number of years and a substantial amount of experience has contributed to the development of this guidance.

Within the BSD series the techniques are organised into groups that cover specific areas of the development process, for example *User Centred Design* which covers all aspects of the investigation, specification and design of the user interface.

The techniques provide a practical approach to the analysis and design of IT systems. They can also be used in conjunction with other complementary techniques such as Object-Oriented techniques.

The material used within this series originated in the Structured Systems Analysis and Design Method (SSADM) which was introduced by the CCTA as a standard method for the development of medium to large IT systems. Since its introduction in the early 1980's, SSADM has been developed through a number of versions to keep pace with the evolving technology and approaches in the IT industry.

The *SSADM Foundation* volume within the BSD series describes the basic concepts of the method and the way in which it can be employed on projects. It also describes how the different techniques can be used in combination. Each of the other volumes in the series describes techniques and approaches for developing elements of the overall specification and design. These can be used in conjunction with one another or as part of alternative approaches. Cross-referencing is provided in outline within the description of each of the techniques to give pointers to the other approaches and techniques that should be considered for use in combination with the one being described.

All volumes within the Business System Development series are available from:

The Stationery Office
St Crispins
Duke Street
Norwich
NR3 1PD

Acknowledgments

Laurence Slater of Slater Consulting Ltd is acknowledged for editing existing material and where necessary developing new material for the volumes within the Business Systems Development series. John Hall, Jennifer Stapleton, Caroline Slater and Ian Clowes are acknowledged for much of the original material on which this series is based.

The following are thanked for their contribution and co-operation in the development of this series:

Paul Turner	-	Parity Training
Tony Jenkins	-	Parity Training
Caroline Slater	-	Slater Consulting Ltd

In addition to those named above a number of people agreed to review aspects of the series and they are thanked accordingly.

1   INTRODUCTION TO THIS VOLUME

The purpose of Physical Design is to specify the physical data and processes for the new system using the language and features of the chosen physical environment and incorporating installation standards. The integrity of the Logical Design is maintained as far as possible, whilst exploiting the strengths of the implementation products and minimising their weaknesses. Essential performance requirements are also addressed.

Physical Design consists of two activities:

- **Database Design**, in which the Logical Data Model for the new system is turned into a physical design which is architecturally correct. Often this task actually involves the building of the database itself.

- **Physical Process Specification**, in which the products of the Logical Design which contain elements of processing (e.g., functions) are used to produce a environment specific process specifications. These are often known as Program Specifications.

Following Physical Design, no further specification or design activity should be necessary to enable the system to be developed. Indeed, it is probable that a significant proportion of components will have already been constructed.

The products of Physical Design are a mapping of the logical design products developed earlier in the project onto the physical environment, in accordance with any installation standards. This mapping will rarely be a direct translation of the logical design products onto their physical equivalents. Instead, it will usually be necessary to change some elements of them in order to take advantage of features of the technology and to ensure that performance objectives are met. Optimising the Physical Design will require trade-offs between factors such as space, performance, ease of use, portability and maintainability. Any change should be as the result of conscious decisions and should be documented.

Physical Design should not in itself alter the Logical Design. However, if, during Physical Design, flaws in the Logical Design are revealed, the designers should revise the Logical Design and work forward from there. It is important to retain a logical specification distinct from its mapping onto a specific technology as this can be used during maintenance of the system and can be a useful starting point if the need arises to implement the same system on a different platform.

Physical Design and the System Development Template

In this series all products are shown in the context of the System Development Template (SDT). This is a template that divides the system development process into activity areas onto which the development products can be mapped. Annexe A provides a fuller description of the System Development Template.

The relationship of Physical Design with the System Development Template is slightly more complicated than with other areas of analysis and design. This is represented in Figure 1-1.

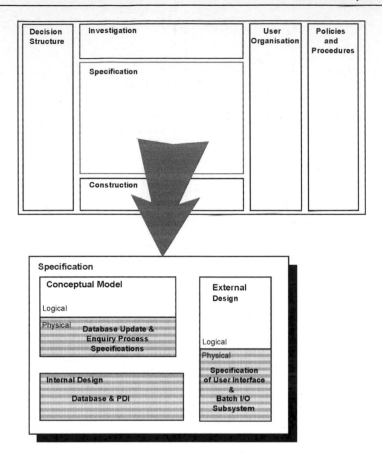

Figure 1-1 Physical Design in the System Development Template

Within Specification, Physical Design contains elements of all three of its constituent components. The Conceptual Model and External Design have both logical and physical parts.

Figure 1-2 represents the fact that all three components of Specification will need to be mapped onto a Physical Design.

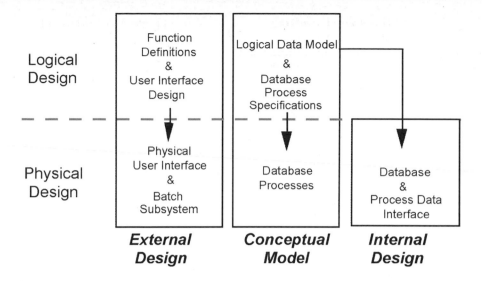

Figure 1-2 Logical to Physical mapping

Organisation of this volume

After this (introductory) chapter the volume is organised as follows.

Chapter 2 – Introduction to Physical Design. This chapter gives a introduction to the overall principles of Physical Design and introduces the two different areas of Physical Design (Database Design and Physical Process Specifications).

Chapter 3 – Database Design. This chapter provides a full description of the products and techniques of Database Design and shows how the Logical Data Model can be turned into architecture specific Database Design.

Chapter 4 – Physical Process Design. This chapter gives the various principles of development of Physical Process Specifications (Program Specifications) and shows which of the logical design products should be used to derive them.

Chapter 5 – Product Descriptions. Product descriptions are provided for all the major products described in this volume. These should be used by projects as a basis for the product descriptions to be used on the project. (Note: It is expected that the project will need to tailor these product descriptions so that items not required are omitted and any other items required by the project included.)

Annexes. There are three annexes appended to this volume. The first gives a description of the System Development Template, the second is a description of EU-Rent which is the case study that is used throughout this volume. The third is a glossary of terms that are relevant to this volume.

2   OVERVIEW OF PHYSICAL DESIGN

The guidance given in this area is different from the guidance given for other techniques in this series. It is not possible to be specific about the way in which the Logical Design is mapped onto specific technologies. This will be different for each different type of environment. Also, the standards adopted by individual organisations will influence the practice of Physical Design. This is summarised in Figure 2-1.

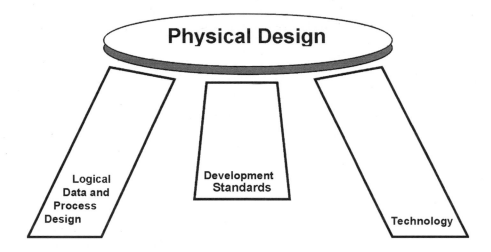

Figure 2-1 Requirements for Physical Design

In order to produce a coherent Physical Design, it is necessary to understand all three elements. The approach to Physical Design must be devised to incorporate the specific features of the implementation technology and the development standards.

The basic process of Physical Design is described in this volume as follows:

- prepare for Physical Design:
    - learn the rules of the implementation environment;
    - review the precise requirements for logical to physical mapping;
    - plan the approach.
- complete the specification of functions;
- incrementally and iteratively develop the data and process designs using a cycle of:
    - design;
    - test against objectives;
    - optimise;
    - review.

2.1   Preparing for Physical Design

Preparation for Physical Design can be initiated as soon as the implementation environment and technology have been determined. Both preparation and implementation will vary from project to project depending upon:

- procurement issues;
- local standards and technical policies of the organisation;
- the existence of other parallel and related projects;
- the timing of Technical System Options (see the *SSADM Foundation* volume in this series).

2.2   Physical Design Strategy

This volume provides a general approach to Physical Design, aimed at a range of implementation environments rather than a specific one. Nevertheless, without compromising the Logical Design, the Physical Design needs to exploit the benefits and circumvent the constraints of the chosen implementation environment.

Physical Design includes the definition of a strategy for implementing the Logical Design in a specific environment, stating how best to use the facilities provided by that environment. The Physical Design Strategy is based on a general classification scheme which identifies the major data handling, performance and processing characteristics of the target environment.

The explanation of how to use the features of a specific product may be provided (in full or in part) by the product supplier. With or without these details, it is imperative that the Physical Design team have or develop expertise in the use of the specific implementation products.

2.3   Database Design

The scope of the term Database Design is very broad. In this volume, the term refers specifically to the study of the complex issues of:

- physical data placement;
- DBMS optimisation.

This volume provides general rules of thumb applicable to most DBMSs or file handlers for quickly producing an initial physical data model. Product specific rules can then be applied. Timing and sizing is carried out on the design and, if necessary, changes are made to the design to meet performance and space objectives. Chapter 3 gives a full description of Database Design.

2.4   Physical Process Design

The Logical Design may not be at a sufficient level of completeness or detail for direct implementation in a physical environment. For example, it may not contain full details of the processing associated with the reporting and correcting of syntax errors.

In Physical Design, after completing the Logical Design, the designer carries out program specification and design, based on the Function Component Implementation Map (FCIM), which specifies the packaging of processing components into units for implementation and the relationships between these units, including reuse. Activities include:

- physical specification of the external design, including GUI interfaces, batch input - output programs, transient files;

- physical specification of the conceptual model, including update and enquiry processes and (if applicable) automated business activities.

- the Process-Data Interface (PDI), which hides the physical database design from the conceptual model, and allows update and enquiry processes to be written as if they accessed the Logical Data Model.

Chapter 4 gives a full description of Physical Process Design.

2.5   Physical Design Issues

2.5.1 *The overlap between process and data design*

The Logical Data Model is a convenient way of exploring and specifying business rules governing the updating and deletion of stored data since it provides the basis for communicating with the user about data. For example, in Entity Life History Analysis, some of the rules expressed in the Logical Data Structure are also represented in Entity Life Histories. The rules expressed in Entity Life Histories and the constraints expressed in the Required System LDM are later represented in Conceptual Process Modelling products.

Some DBMSs, fourth generation languages and dictionaries support declarative methods for describing some of the business rules or constraints (e.g., validation of input data items, referential integrity checks), from which they can automatically generate triggers, stored procedures and process code. When producing Physical Process Designs it is important to recognise the capabilities of the software and avoid unnecessary work in specification, programming and testing.

2.5.2 *Contradictory requirements in Database Design*

The design of a database supports many, potentially incompatible, requirements. In theory, the designer could attempt to minimise:

- data access times and processor utilisation (to minimise run times and response times, or reduce accounting costs on a shared system, or both);

- the requirements for backing store;

- the system development time;

- the system maintenance time;

- the risk of database reorganisation (especially where data or transaction volumes do not occur as predicted);

- the complexity of the system/user interface (especially for users who use the ad hoc query facilities of a package which operates directly on the physical records).

These requirements are likely to be contradictory. Thus, there is unlikely to be an optimum answer to any physical database design problem. The designer should therefore only optimise to meet essential requirements.

Before planning an approach to the design, the designer and the user must assess what importance they place on the various requirements. Even though requirements have had priorities assigned, it is not possible to evaluate designs using a simple weighted ranking scheme. Marginal gains in one area must be assessed against losses in another.

The approach taken in this volume is to establish some general principles for assigning priorities and only investigate more deeply if the design cannot be accomplished within those principles. This approach is based on the fact that during the last thirty years, hardware costs have fallen dramatically and continue to fall, whilst staff costs have risen and continue to rise. This leads to a design based on the following assumptions:

- backing storage costs are of secondary importance;

- run times and response times should be minimised (though for human interface reasons rather than computer cost reasons);

- design, programming and maintenance staff costs should be minimised;

- end-user interfaces to physical data should be as simple as possible.

To meet these requirements, the approach described depends on trying to restrict the usage of physical data storage mechanisms to those where there is a one-to-one mapping between logical and physical data.

2.5.3 One-to-one mapping

An objective of Database Design is to produce a one-to-one mapping between logical and physical data. If this is achieved, no special programming will be required to maintain redundant data or to reassemble logical records from fragmented physical records. End-user query facilities can also operate on physical records which look exactly like the logical records.

If there is anything other than a direct one-to-one mapping between the logical concepts and their physical representations in the database, then at Physical Design there are two strategies which may be adopted. The designer may:

- examine the Conceptual Process Modelling products and amend them where necessary to handle the physical database;

- implement the Conceptual Process Modelling products as they are, and develop a Process Data Interface to sit between the logical database processes (which are implemented as if they accessed the Logical Data Model) and the physical database.

2.5.4 The Process Data Interface (PDI)

A Process Data Interface sits between the physical database and the implemented database update and enquiry processes. With a Process Data Interface, database updates and enquiries are implemented as if they accessed the Logical Data Model. The Process Data Interface accepts 'logical' read, write, create and delete operations and carries out the equivalent physical accesses. Note that this does not necessarily imply run-time interpretation of data access operations; a Process Data Interface could be as simple as a set of source code entries for physical data accesses, placed in a library by a database administrator and included in database update and enquiry processes at compilation time.

The Process Data Interface is quite often implemented as a piece of 'middleware'.

It should be noted that it is possible to have a 'null' Process Data Interface in which case all the Physical Process Specifications will directly access the database.

If the Database Design changes, the Process Data Interface is amended to map the Logical Data Model onto the new Database Design. Update and enquiry processing does not need to change (other than, perhaps, recompilation to include the updated Database Design). Physical design changes might include:

- restructuring of the database to improve performance or to exploit features in future releases of the DBMS;

- changing the distribution, partitioning or replication of data;

- moving the database to a different DBMS. A variant of this is that a Process Data Interface can provide access to data in legacy systems which can then be migrated into new databases.

Also, if users, who have an understanding of the Logical Data Model, are to be involved in specifying database queries, then it is important that they are able to do this without worrying about the physical structure of the database or file store. Users should be able to specify database processes as though the Required System Logical Data Model is the database.

The Process Data Interface is represented in Figure 2-2.

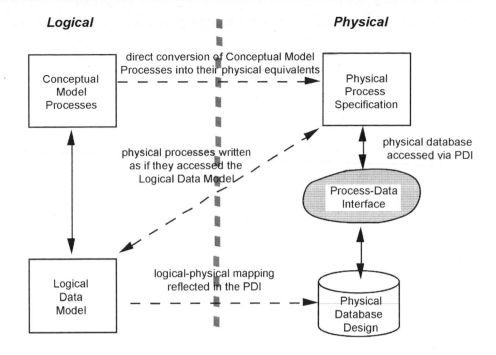

Figure 2-2 The Process Data Interface

Implementation of the Process Data Interface may involve using code to support 'logical views' (whether in COBOL or special-purpose languages such as SQL). Alternatively, it may involve data dictionary languages and facilities.

There are four main technical reasons for developing a Process Data Interface. It facilitates:

- documentation of the design path;
- efficiency;
- economy;
- logical/physical data independence.

There are also technical policy reasons. For example, a technical policy may define a specific role for data administration leading to a requirement to use dictionary facilities for standard definitions of data formats, domains, views and access paths.

The Required System Logical Data Model enables the user and the analyst to answer important questions about information requirements, without needing to consider physical implementation and performance constraints.

2.5.5 Function Component Implementation Map

The Function Component Implementation Map supports overall control of specification of physical processing. It specifies:

- grouping of logical specification components into physical components for implementation and testing;

- the relationships between physical components, including reuse.

Creation of the Function Component Implementation Map is concerned with identifying logical components that can be grouped together to form physical units, taking account of:

- reusability of components;

- mapping to the technical architecture; for example, ensuring that client and server processes are developed separately;

- mapping to technical platforms; for example, individual window specifications that have to be implemented on more than one type of workstation.

Note that the physical components defined may, after programming and testing, be bound into larger run-units for the implemented system.

The Function Component Implementation Map is then used:

- as the basis for production of detailed specifications of components, to be handed over to implementers;

- to support testing and integration;

- as a primary product for analysis of impact of requested changes during system maintenance.

How the Function Component Implementation Map is itself implemented will depend on the repository or dictionary facilities available. It may be necessary to set up a small database specifically for it with cross-references to logical and physical components in the CASE tool repository and the implementation code libraries.

3   DATABASE DESIGN

Database Design is concerned with the physical placement of data and the impact that this placement has on access to the data. Database Design is a complex subject and is not covered comprehensively in this volume. Additional skills and knowledge about the technical environment and the data management software are needed.

This chapter describes Database Design from the perspective of two groups of people:

- analysts who will be responsible for providing database designers with information about the requirements for data design. This chapter should provide this group with knowledge of which products are important for Database Design and an appreciation of what the database designer and database administrator will be doing with these products;

- database designers and database administrators who need to know how to use logical design products. This chapter should provide this group with an appreciation of the role of the Process Data Interface (PDI) and the need for synchronisation between process and data design.

Database Design is in the Internal Design area of the System Development Template as shown in Figure 3-1.

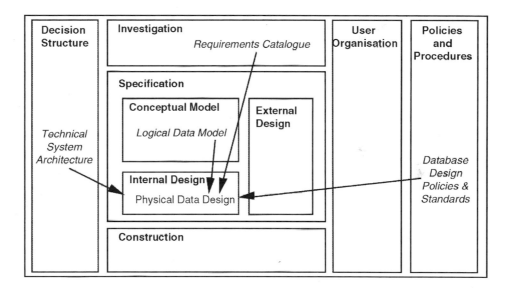

Figure 3-1 Database Design in the System Development Template

The objective of Database Design is to develop a design which:

- implements the new system's data requirements, as defined in the Required System Logical Data Model;

- supports the system's processing requirements;

- meets the space and timing objectives set for the system.

In many installations practitioners do not undertake the actual database design and optimisation – this is done by specialist database designers. This chapter should provide practitioners with an appreciation of what is done in database design, but if they are required to design the database on a project, it will not provide all the information necessary. Additional, product-specific training will be needed.

Database Design Considerations

In developing a Database Design the following must be addressed:

- to produce an efficient Database Design from a Logical Data Model, the designer must have a thorough understanding of the chosen implementation environment;

- the designer needs to know how far to optimise the design. The aim is to produce a design that is good enough to meet the system performance objectives;

- system performance objectives may conflict with other requirements, for example, maintainability, development time, storage constraints, etc.

To tackle these problems the Database Design technique provides a general framework for the design team to follow. This can be tailored as necessary. If the design team follows the this framework the database designer is required to perform the following activities:

- define a strategy to be followed in Database Design;

- produce a Database Design;

- test and optimise the Database Design where necessary, to meet the performance objectives.

In order to do this, the database designer may need to first gain an understanding of the implementation environment and identify facilities and constraints within the implementation environment which will have an impact on the production of the physical specification.

The Database design technique outlined in this chapter is mostly designed for data processing type databases which are in general use. Other types of database exist, namely:

- Object-oriented and hybrid databases;

- Multimedia databases;

- Web-enabled databases;

- Data warehouses.

For these types of databases, the technique outlined in this chapter will need to be supplemented with expert knowledge in that type of database.

3.1   Database Design Products

The final product of Database Design is the Database Design.

During the conduct of Database Design, a number of intermediate products may be produced to assist the database designer. These intermediate products may be provided from outside the project or may be developed specifically for the project and may include:

- **Physical Design Strategy**. In organisations where a new Database Management System (DBMS) is being introduced or this is the first project to implement a database on the DBMS, it may be useful to develop a strategy for Database Design. In many cases, the method for database design will be well established within the organisation;

- **DBMS classifications**. From descriptions of the database facilities and features, it may be useful to develop a classification of data storage characteristics and performance;

- **Space and Timing estimation spreadsheets**. These can be used to check whether the Database Design is likely to meet space and timing objectives. They can be used during optimisation of the design.

3.2   Database Design Overview

A Required System Logical Data Model (see the *Data Modelling* volume in this series) is an implementation-independent design. When an implementation environment has been selected, the Required System Logical Data Model must be transformed into a database or file design which is expressed in terms of the physical storage and access facilities provided in that implementation environment.

Figure 3-2 gives an overview of Database Design as described in this chapter.

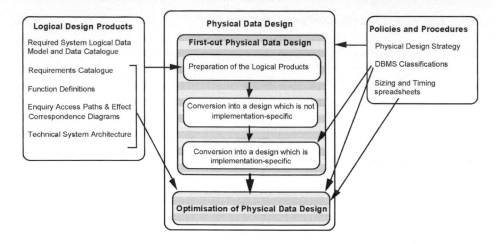

Figure 3-2 Overview of Database Design

The individual steps are described in detail in the following sections the last of which gives an example from the EU-Rent case study.

3.3   Creating the initial Database Design (first-cut)

This section describes how the Database Design is developed from the Required System Logical Data Model. This design is implementable on the target DBMS, but it has not been tested to determine if the service level requirements for the system functions could be met using this design. This first attempt at producing a Database Design is known as first-cut.

3.3.1 General objectives of first-cut data design

The Required System Logical Data Model is a logical model and does not describe the physical files in which entity data is stored: apart from volumes of entity instances, it has no physical or performance characteristics.

In first-cut data design the main objectives are to produce a Database Design:

- which is realistic enough for performance prediction;
- swiftly, using simple rules of thumb;
- which minimises programming costs.

These objectives are reached by making a series of transformations to the Required System Logical Data Model to finally produce a Database Design. It should be noted the Required System Logical Data Model still exists in its own right: the Database Design does not replace it.

3.3.2 Assumptions about DBMS Facilities

In developing a first-cut data design, there are certain principles which will tend to be true whichever DBMS is targeted. These general principles can be stated as assumptions about DBMSs which makes first-cut data design similar for a wide variety of DBMSs.

Entities are represented as record types

The unit of logical access is a record. Each entity occurrence (with attributes) will be implemented as a record (with data items). In addition, entity aspect occurrences may be implemented as records within different tables or entity aspects may be implemented as different views of a single table.

Records are stored on blocks

The unit of physical access is a block (or page). Most DBMSs offer some facilities for controlling the placement of records in blocks; accessing related records in the same block more efficiently than records in other blocks; allowing for space for expansion of records within blocks.

Records are grouped into physical groups

Data that is likely to be accessed as a group frequently or with high performance requirements needs to be stored together as a group. So, groups of details for the same master should be clustered together; there may also be possibilities of placing such a group near its master.

This means that the data design needs to be based around a set of physical groups of masters, details, details of details, etc., whose placement on disk blocks can be specified within the DBMS. These physical groups represent a hierarchy drawn from the Required System Logical Data Model.

It should be noted that the concept of physical grouping related data is useful in Database Design, even if hierarchies are not specifically supported within the DBMS.

Primary relationships within a physical group are supported

Relationships in the Required System Logical Data Model which exist between master and detail entity records in the same physical group are known as primary relationships. The DBMS will usually offer good support for these relationships.

For example, most DBMSs provide some facility whereby 'Read next detail of current master' is more efficient within a physical group than between physical groups.

Secondary relationships between physical groups are supported

Other relationships, between records in different physical groups, are known as secondary relationships. These sometimes need to be implemented in the DBMS-specific design by means of a different mechanism from that used by the DBMS for the primary relationships, and may be subject to special restrictions (e.g., requirement for a full index, where there might be an option to use a partial or compressed index to access records via their 'grouped by' key).

Assumes all data is centralised

For the first-cut database design it is assumed that all the data will be held centrally and not split up.

3.3.3 First-cut Database Design activities

The Database Design is produced in three broad activities:

- preparation of the logical design products;
- conversion into a design which is not implementation-specific;
- conversion into a design which is implementation-specific.

These activities are described further in the following paragraphs.

Preparation of the Logical Design products

As the scope of Database Design is limited, not all the information recorded on the Required System Logical Data Model is required for Database Design. The differences between the information provided by the Required System Logical Data Structure and that needed in Database Design are as follows:

- the relationship names on the Required System Logical Data Structure are not used in Database Design (although it should be noted that physical relationship names may need to be provided eventually for the target DBMS);
- the only facet of relationship optionality required for Database Design is whether or not a master must exist for a detail (only mandatory detail to master relationships are used to determine the placing of non-root entities in physical groups);
- the implementation of exclusion arcs on relationships does not affect Database Design where the scope is limited to the placement and accessing of data.

This means that a simple starting point for database design can be derived from the Required System Logical Data Model by:

- removing relationship names;
- dealing with each type hierarchy in one of two ways:
    - if sub-types have few distinct attributes, roll them up into the super-type; the resulting record will require a 'sub-type' attribute, and will have some attributes that are mutually exclusive, depending on the value of the sub-type attribute;
    - if sub-types have many distinct attributes, make them separate record types with the same key as the super-type.

- denoting optionality only from detail to master (not master to detail);

- replacing exclusive arcs with optional relationships;

- grouping different aspects of the same real-world entity into a single record type.

An example Logical Data Model is shown in Figure 3-3.

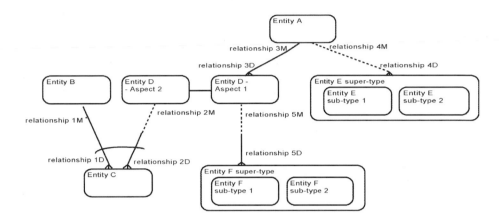

Figure 3-3 Example Logical Data Model

Application of the guidelines given above for preparation of the Logical Data Model results in the model shown in Figure 3-4.

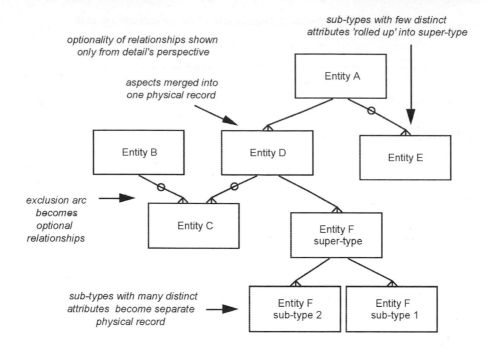

Figure 3-4 Preparation of Logical Data Model for Physical Design

Design volumes must be carried over from the Required System Logical Data Model to the physical data model. The design volumes are the number of occurrences of each entity (shown in each entity box) and the dependent occurrences, how many details there are per master (shown by numbers on the crow's feet).

Non-key entry points need to be identified. The access entry points can be derived from the Effect Correspondence Diagrams (ECDs) and Enquiry Access Paths (EAPs). To identify the non-key entry points it is necessary to:

- identify the required access entry points on the data model;
- compare the data items on each access entry point with the data items in the key of the entity being accessed to identify those which do not match (i.e., non-key entry points);
- distinguish these non-key entry points from the entry points via the primary key.

Conversion into a design which is not implementation-specific

On the early data design developed in the previous activity, it is useful to identify the roots of what will become physical groups. Two kinds of entity are identified as the root of a physical group:

- entities without any master in the data model;
- entities used as a direct access entry point, unless

- its key includes the key of one of its master entities, and

- that master entity is already the top of a group.

Each root entity should be annotated in some way on the data design.

The allowable or valid physical groups for each non-root entity are then identified.

- a non-root entity can only be placed in a physical group if one of its mandatory masters has been placed in that physical group;

- if a non-root entity is a direct access point and there is a choice of which physical group to place it in (i.e. it has more than one mandatory master in different groups), it should be placed with the master whose key is part of its own key.

If it is valid to place an entity in more than one physical group, because more than one allowable physical group has been identified, then the least dependent occurrence rule is used to decide in which group to place the entity.

The least dependent occurrence rule states that when it is possible to store an entity in two or more physical hierarchies it should be stored in the one in which it has fewest occurrences. The least dependent occurrence rule is only a rule of thumb, which nevertheless produces acceptable results in most situations.

Conversion into a design which is implementation specific

This activity will be undertaken by the database designer/database administrator.

The designer:

- decides in detail which facilities, from those provided by the target DBMS, are to be used to produce the Database Design;

- converts the first-cut design which is based on general features to a product specific design using product specific rules.

Estimation of the space needed is a important activity, for which it will be necessary to divide the design into blocks. There are several factors which affect the choice of block size for the first-cut Database Design:

- block sizes supported by the DBMS;

- the sizes of the most commonly used groups;

- DBMS overheads;

- the amount of space the blocks will take up when read into memory.

The aim is to choose a block size that accommodates the largest of the commonly used groups. These commonly used groups can be determined from the Function Definitions and their associated Enquiry Access Paths and Effect Correspondence Diagrams. The Function Definitions document not only the frequency of the function but also the frequency of the components, the events and the enquiries.

The block size chosen must be supported by the target DBMS and the blocks must not be so large that the size of buffers needed to read them causes memory problems when a number of transactions hit the system at once.

Once the block size has been decided the physical groups can be checked against it. The size of the data in each record is calculated by adding up the lengths of the data items in the entity descriptions. It is also necessary to make some assumptions about the costs of maintaining relationships and the costs of the management of disk space.

When a physical group will not fit into a block the physical group will need to be split into two or more smaller groups.

Once the physical blocks have been identified, it will be necessary for the database designer to decide how to use the mechanisms of the DBMS to implement the data design in the most optimal way.

3.4   Optimising the Database Design

The database designer/database administrator needs to apply optimisation techniques to the Database Design in a controlled way in order to meet preset performance objectives. Here, some general guidance is given on optimising a Database Design and some general principles are described. Projects will need to decide on the most appropriate way to optimise their Database Designs, based upon expert advice.

Whilst some environments permit the easy generation of a database from a design so that timings can be assessed by benchmarks, this volume only describes a generic approach of estimation based on the design.

There are two principles used in this volume to moderate the optimisation process:

- Optimise only in order to achieve preset performance objectives. Optimisation helps to save space (in terms of data storage) and/or time (in terms of processing speed).

- Preserve the Logical Data Model as much as possible. The closer the implemented system is to the Logical Data Model, the easier it will be to understand and maintain.

A systematic optimisation process should be applied to the product specific design in order to ensure that the performance objectives of the system can be met. This process is an iterative one, as shown in Figure 3-5.

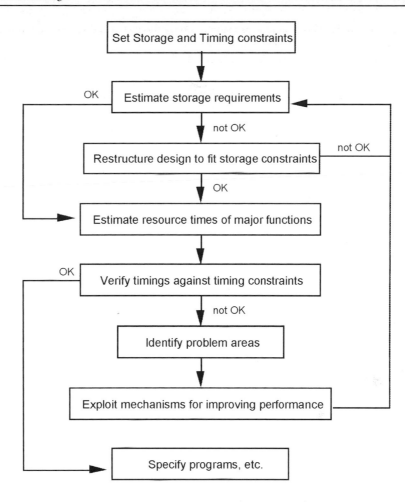

Figure 3-5 Database Design optimisation approach

The designer should stop when a design meets the objectives. It is important not to over-design, nor to waste resources trying to meet a constraint which does not exist. It also means that if a solution which meets the existing constraints is complex, the designer should be prepared to talk to the users about relaxing those constraints.

Where the constraints cannot be met they must be reviewed by the users and modified.

Set Storage and Timing constraints

Storage and Timing constraints can be derived from the requirements in the Requirements Catalogue, particularly the non-functional requirements.

If the Database Design meets the original constraints, then it will be implemented as directly as possible. If not, then it will be optimised to reduce storage space and/or processing time.

Estimate storage requirements

At this point the size of each physical group type is multiplied by the number of instances of that physical group and the results are accumulated as a basis for estimating the overall size requirements for the database. The size of each physical group should be increased substantially to allow for load factors and security requirements.

To estimate the size of each group the designer may wish to use space estimation spreadsheets, which facilitate the calculation of record sizes, accounting for indexes, pointer chains, etc.

Restructure design to fit storage constraints

Storage constraints usually have only a minor impact on the final design. If storage constraints are a problem, there are several mechanisms which can be exploited to alleviate this:

- preserving one-to-one mapping. This might involve:
    - distributing the data better;
    - compressing the data.
- not preserving one-to-one mapping. This might involve:
    - compressing data;
    - removing redundant data;
    - reducing historical data.
- other ways to save space can be used including mechanisms to improve performance (e.g., change access method, adjust block size) used in reverse, to save space.

Timing and Storage may need to be traded off against each other.

Estimate resource times of major functions

The high-resource consuming functions can be identified quite easily. They are almost always the ones that hit or create the entities with the most number of occurrences – usually the entities near the bottom of the Logical Data Model.

Only the major functions should be used here, as small a number as possible.

The designer should examine the first-cut design to see which physical records need to be accessed to support the logical accesses required by a critical function.

The designer is likely to use a timing estimation spreadsheet. This spreadsheet can now be populated:

- record the physical access information (the record types to be accessed, the number accessed, access type and the access path);

- record the disk accesses required to make the physical reads and writes. The designer must identify how many disk accesses are caused by the DBMS reads and writes. For example, most DBMSs will not re-read a block that has already been accessed in order to retrieve a more-or-less immediately previously required record.

Identify problem areas

The timing estimation spreadsheet results are compared with the performance objectives. Attention should be focused on large numbers of disk accesses.

For any problems identified by this comparison there are usually only a very limited number of options. This is an advantage, not a disadvantage, as effort is concentrated on a limited number of likely solutions.

Exploit mechanisms for improving performance

It is possible to improve performance by retaining the structure of the Conceptual Model, and using DBMS facilities to improve performance. In this case, it is useful to perform estimates for all critical functions before attempting to improve any of them.

Techniques to be considered (where the selected DBMS supports them) are:

- optimise storage of entities by:
    - placing details near masters whose relationship is most often used;
    - changing the access method (hashed to indexed or vice-versa, etc.);
    - implementing key-only entities as indexes or vice-versa;
    - adding direct access mechanisms to detail records.
- optimise storage of relationships by:
    - using different options for indexing (e.g., partial index for clustered records, compressed index);
    - adding forward, backward and owner pointers;
    - sorting by key or other data items.
- reduce database disk accesses by holding hold reference (look-up) tables in store;
- use partitioning or replication facilities within the DBMS to reduce the volume of data held on the central server and to place data near to its end-user's processing resources. Current best practice suggests that only non-volatile data should be subject to partitioning and/or replication;
- reduce processing times by holding some of the derived values.

When changes are made to the design to meet performance objectives for one function the designer must ensure that the other functions still meet their objectives.

In addition there are other Database Design tactics which do not impact upon the one-to-one mapping:

- adjust block size;

- adjust number of blocks in buffer pool;

- adjust packing density;

- move most active data to faster devices;

- hold frequently accessed blocks of database in buffer – minimise DBMS overhead;

- optimise disk placement of files;

- copy database for retrieval only (if done off-line).

It is also possible to improve performance by compromising the structure of the Logical Data Model or by not using DBMS facilities.

3.5   Completing the Database Design

Validate the impact of any imposed sequencing

If sorting is used to improve performance the sorted transactions may access the relevant entities in a different sequence from that in which they occurred in the real world. Most of the time there will be no problem. If there is a problem the relevant part of the design must be reworked.

Identify any processing optimisation requirements

It may not be possible to meet all performance objectives using the data design techniques described above. Performance can also be improved by improving the efficiency of code, for example, service routines may be written in assembler.

Update the service level requirements

The designer may have to agree with the user to reduce service level requirements either because there are conflicting performance objectives for different functions or because it is difficult to meet the objectives.

Plan to use contiguity to represent primary relationships

Because the records in physical groups are stored close together in the file details can always be quickly accessed sequentially from masters. Masters can be accessed directly by key (if stored in the detail record) or by pointer.

3.6   EU-Rent Example

The following is an example of Database Design for EU-Rent.

The selected Technical System Option (see the *SSADM Foundation* volume in this series) consists of two hierarchical client-server designs, for rentals and for maintenance, plus a head office system for administering the customer benefits programme and maintaining reference data.

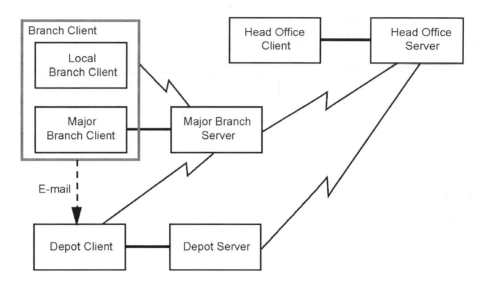

Figure 3-6 EU-Rent System

3.6.1 EU-Rent Database Design Policies

This section gives the policies that are used, within EU-Rent, for database design.

DBMS Classification

The DBMS is relational. It can be accessed by means of:

- interactive SQL;
- embedded SQL, in a range of host languages including C and COBOL;
- a direct forms interface;
- database triggers – processes attached to reads and updates of specified tables and invoked automatically when those reads or updates take place.

The DBMS does not support data location transparency; both database calls and stored procedure calls may be remote, but the calling program has to specify the call destination.

The DBMS does not recognise data replication; if data is replicated, the application programs are responsible for updating all copies.

The DBMS has no facilities for handling sub-types automatically.

Placement options

Rows can be clustered by one key, which does not have to be the primary key (see Access, below). The clustering key may have multiple parts, not necessarily contiguous columns.

Hierarchies of tables can be mapped to blocks of storage, i.e., a master and its details can physically be stored in the same disk block, but are managed as separate tables for data access by programs. Hierarchies may be indefinitely deep, although it is recommended that hierarchy occurrences should be smaller than the disk blocks they are stored in; handling of overflow is fairly inefficient in this DBMS.

In a hierarchy, the system will maintain a mandatory index on the master by the key used for the relationship.

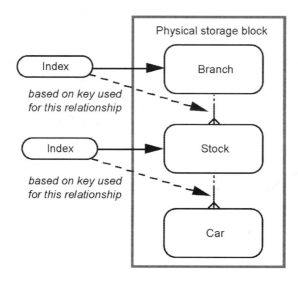

The DBMS supports specification of a hierarchy of tables that are distinct for programming, but stored so that related rows for each are in the same physical block.

The master will be indexed on the key used to support the relationship on which hierarchical storage is based (usually the primary key of the master).

Figure 3-7 Hierarchical physical storage of related tables

Block sizes of 2k, 4k, 8k, 16k, 32k and 64k bytes are supported. The recommended block size is 4k for data and 2k for index. Different tables in the same database may have different block sizes.

Implementation of relationship

Relationships are implemented by keys – compound, hierarchical and/or foreign.

Relationships may be supported by indexes, which can be created or dropped after implementation.

'Downward' referential integrity is supported for deletion – 'cascade', 'restrict' and 'set null' options for details when a master is deleted, one option per detail table. If referential integrity is turned on, the DBMS will maintain a mandatory index by the master's key on the detail. Other referential integrity requirements, e.g., 'master must be present for creation of detail', 'master must have at least one detail', 'cascade, restrict and set null apply to different subsets of the detail, depending on state', can be supported by 'triggers' (custom procedures attached to database reads and writes).

Access

Each table must have a primary key, whose values uniquely identify rows. The DBMS will maintain a mandatory index by primary key for all tables except for details in a hierarchy where the hierarchy is based on their primary key.

A table may have any number of secondary indexes, which may be based on multiple columns, not necessarily contiguous. A column may be used in multiple indexes.

If an index exists to support retrieval criteria, the DBMS will use it; otherwise it will scan the table for appropriate rows.

If several indexes each provide partial support for retrieval criteria, e.g., 'Select rentals for a given customer and pick-up branch, the DBMS will combine the index entries to identify the required rows before actually retrieving the rows.

Retrieval by cursor is supported, i.e., if multiple rows match selection criteria they can be retrieved one at a time in 'get next' mode; each time a selected row is retrieved the cursor is automatically updated to point to the next selected row.

SQL views are supported, including joined views – i.e. views based on multiple tables (e.g., selected columns of Rental plus Address of Pick-up Branch and Name of Customer).

Restrictions

The only views that are updatable are those based on single tables.

The DBMS does not provide data location or replication transparency. Processes that access remote data need to specify where the required data is. If data is replicated, processes that update it need to update each copy of it.

Triggers and Stored Procedures are not supported by the chosen architecture.

Physical design strategy

The main issues in the design strategy that affect data design are:

Sub-types

The DBMS cannot handle type hierarchies automatically. The first-cut approach is to select one of the following options for each type hierarchy:

- if sub-types have few distinct attributes, roll them up into the super-type; the resulting table will require a 'sub-type' column, and will have some columns that are mutually exclusive, depending on the value in the sub-type column.

  Define an (updateable) SQL view of the table for the supertype and each sub-type. Database update and enquiry processes will operate on these views.

- if sub-types have many distinct attributes, make the super-type and each sub-type into a separate table; include the super-type key in each table.

A third option may be used, if required, to improve performance: the super-type may be rolled down into the sub-types – a separate table is created for each sub-type and the super-type columns replicated in each sub-type table. The trade-off is that database update and enquiry processes for the super-type will no longer be physically reusable (since SQL accesses are specified only for a single table or view, and the DBMS does not support updating of a joined view); separate copies would have to be made for each sub-type table.

Data location

History data should not be moved until it is needed.

For example, a depot will need a car's service history for maintenance, but the car may move between branches many times between services, and those branches may be served by different depots. The car's service history should not be moved when the car changes branches. Instead, when a service is scheduled, the depot should check whether it has the car's service history, and if it does not, it must then request it (via the head office system) from whichever depot has it.

Managing this kind of data movement cost-effectively may require derived data to be maintained in some entities. For example, storing 'depot at which last service was carried out' in Car (derived from Depot of Branch that owns Car when Service Booking is created) would save a trace through the history of transfers since the car was last serviced.

Data replication

Generally, operational data should not be replicated (although performance may require that some will be).

Small volume, infrequently updated, frequently accessed reference data (such as prices, model descriptions, manufacturer names) should generally be replicated wherever they are needed.

When data is replicated, then, as far as is practical, one copy should be designated the 'primary copy' to which updates are applied and then promulgated to other copies.

Robustness

Locations should be able to provide basic IT support for the business, even when they are isolated from the rest of the network.

Referential integrity

Support for referential integrity is limited (only 'downward on delete') in the DBMS, and incurs the overheads of mandatory indexes.

In general, referential integrity should be turned off unless there are significant performance reasons for letting the DBMS handle it.

Hierarchical physical storage

Hierarchical physical storage (i.e., related rows of different tables stored in the same physical block) should be used only if the relationships on which the hierarchies are based are non-transferable.

Timing and Sizing spreadsheets

Spreadsheets have been developed for estimating data and index space, and for estimating the disk activity for processes.

3.6.2 First-cut Database Design

The EU-Rent Required System Logical Data Model is shown in Figure 3-8.

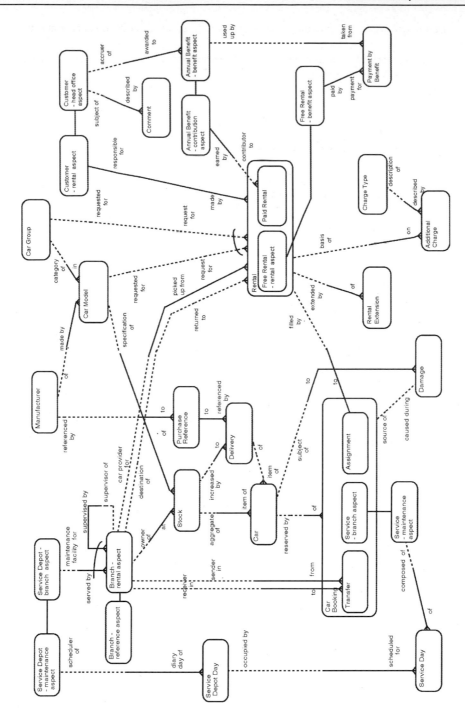

Figure 3-8 EU-Rent Required System Logical Data Model

In the following example only the Database Design for the Branch server is illustrated.

A simple starting point for data design is derived from the Logical Data Model by:

- identifying relevant entities;

- removing relationship names;

- denoting optionality only from detail to master (not master to detail);

- replacing exclusion arcs with optional relationships;

- dealing with sub-types and aspects by rolling them together or defining separate record types.

Applying the above gives the model shown in Figure 3-9.

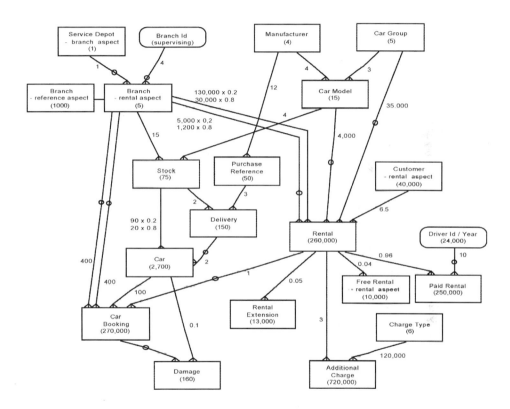

Figure 3-9 EU-Rent Branch Server Physical Data Model

Design volumes are shown as the number of occurrences of each entity (shown in each entity box) and the dependent occurrences, how many details there are per master (shown by numbers on the crow's feet).

Key-only physical entities (which will result, ultimately, in indexes) are shown as narrow, round-cornered boxes.

Volumes

The volumes shown are for servers at major city branches. A server of this type will serve the city branch and three or four local agencies. City branches, in terms of numbers of cars and volumes of business, are about four times the size of a local agency. The split volumes on the Branch-Rentals and Stock-Cars relationships reflect this.

Within an individual server, only its own city Branch and local agency Branches will own Stocks, Rentals and Transfer Bookings. But addresses of all branches will be held on each branch server, for production of directions for transfers and one-way rentals.

Airport branch servers will serve only one branch, and hence will have only fifteen Stocks; otherwise, overall volumes are similar.

Key-only components

The recursive relationship for branch supervision has been replaced by a key-only master of Branch.

On examination, the contribution aspect of Annual Benefit contains only the key and is shown as a key-only master of Paid Rental.

Aspects

Branch has two aspects (one for *rentals* and one for *references*), with five occurrences and 1,000 occurrences. They have been handled as two different record types.

Sub-types

Booking subtypes have few distinct attributes – they have been 'rolled up' with Booking into a single table with a 'sub-type' column and mutually exclusive non-null and the Rental subtypes have significantly different attributes – they have been broken out into separate tables with a common key; see Figure 3-10.

Note: the italics and side-bar notation indicate optional and mutually exclusive fields of the database records. This notation can be used if thought useful.

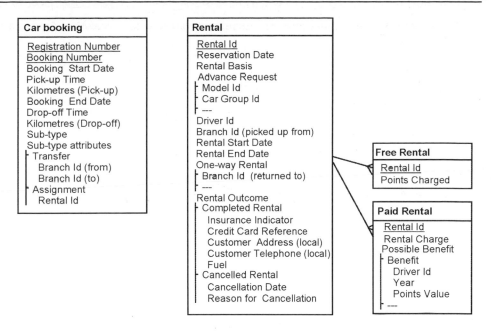

Figure 3-10 Rental Sub-types

3.6.3 *Conversion into a design that is not implementation-specific*

The DBMS selected by EU-Rent supports hierarchical physical storage. The data model has to be partitioned into physical hierarchies. To do this, the entry points and selection criteria are required.

Two kinds of entity are identified as the root of a physical hierarchy:

- any entity without any master in the data model;

- any entity used as a direct access entry point, unless;

  - its key includes the key of one of its master entities, and

  - that master entity is already the top of a group.

The allowable physical hierarchies for each non-root entity are then identified.

- key-only masters and optional relationships (that is, relationships where the detail can exist without being owned by a master) are ignored when specifying hierarchies;

- a non-root entity can only be placed in a physical hierarchy if one of its mandatory masters has been placed in that physical hierarchy;

- if a non-root entity is a direct access point and there is a choice of which physical hierarchy to place it in (i.e., it has more than one mandatory master in different groups) it should be placed with the master whose key is part of its own key.

If, under the guidelines above, an entity could be placed in more than one physical group, the least dependent occurrence rule is used:

"If an entity could be stored in more than one physical hierarchy, place it in the hierarchy in which it will have fewest occurrences."

The least dependent occurrence rule is only a rule of thumb, which nevertheless produces acceptable results in most situations.

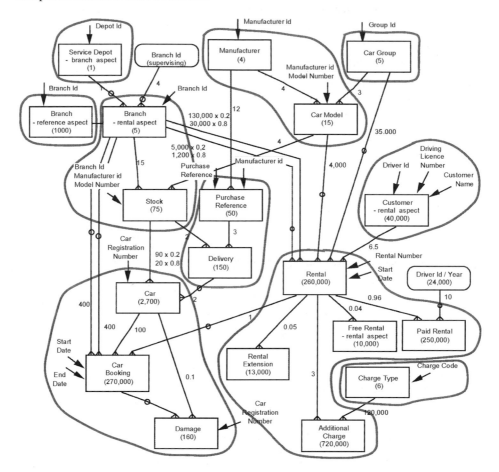

Figure 3-11 Physical Model after Least Dependent Occurrence Rule

3.6.4 Conversion into a design that is implementation specific

At this point product-specific guidelines are needed. For the DBMS selected by EU-Rent they are:

- Each entity type is used to specify a table.

- Hierarchies based on fixed relationships are mapped on to hierarchical storage structure.

- The DBMS will maintain a mandatory primary-key index on all hierarchy roots and stand-alone tables.

- For each table, an index should be created to support each relationship with a master, unless:

    - the table will be small (say, 3 blocks or less);

    - the relationship is maintained by a physical hierarchy.

- If a hierarchy is too large for the selected block size, either:

    - choose a larger block size;

    - split the hierarchy.

The initial product specific model is shown in Figure 3-12.

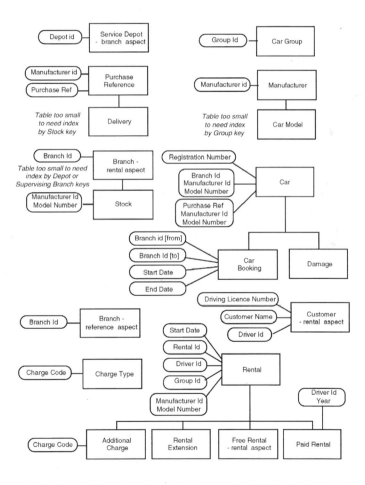

Figure 3-12 Initial Database Design for specific DBMS, before sizing

The structures under Purchase Reference, Branch – rental aspect, Manufacturer, Car and Rental – indicate hierarchical placement. For example, although Car, Car Booking and Damage will be defined as separate tables as far as SQL is concerned, physically they will be organised so that rows of the Car Booking and Damage tables will be placed in the same disk block as their corresponding rows of the Car table.

The design needs to be sized to establish whether the indexes indicated will actually be needed, and if hierarchies will have to be split. A spreadsheet, derived from the technical specification of the DBMS, has been provided. The results are (excluding entities that will obviously lead to very small tables):

Table	Data size	No. of Cols	Row Size	No. of Rows	Block (k)	Dens	Blocks	Space (k)
Branch - rentals	20	3	35	1,000	4	65%	14	56
Branch - reference	170	4	186	1,000	4	65%	72	288
Stock	36	6	54	75	4	65%	2	8
Car	48	8	68	2,700	4	65%	71	284
Booking	92	12	116	270,000	4	65%	12,047	48,188
Customer	41	3	56	40,000	4	65%	862	3,448
Rental	140	16	168	260,000	4	65%	16,800	67,200
Paid Rental	35	6	53	250,000	4	65%	5,097	20,388
Free Rental	18	3	33	10,000	4	65%	127	508
Rental Extension	24	4	40	13,000	4	65%	200	800
Additional Charge	30	4	46	780,000	4	65%	13,800	55,200
							Total	196,368

Figure 3-13 Sizes for DBMS

Notes:

- Data size, number of columns and number of rows are obtained from volumes in the Logical Design products. Data size is an estimate, taking account of data compression (removal of leading zeros and trailing spaces, suppression of null fields).

- Block size and density (the space actually used on file loading or database reorganisation) are defaults that can be overwritten.

- Row size, blocks and space are calculated with formulae derived from the DBMS technical specification, taking account of DBMS overheads.

It is clear that:

- the Car-Booking hierarchy is too large for the block size. Even if we were to double the block size, it would be too big;

- it is not worth creating a index on Stock by Model (Manufacturer Id/Model Number).

There is one other point to be considered. If the number of details per master is greater than the number of disk blocks for the detail table, there is probably no benefit in having an index (although use of a clustering index may be investigated in optimisation). There are 120,000 Additional Charges per Charge Type, spread over 13,800 disk blocks; the index can be dropped.

The revised physical design is shown in Figure 3-14.

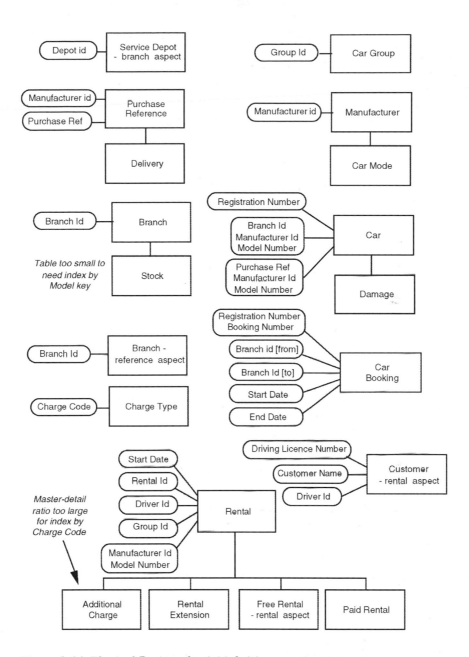

Figure 3-14 Physical Design after initial sizing

To complete the sizing there is a spreadsheet for index sizing:

Table	Index	Key Size	Key Values	Rows per key	Block (k)	Dens	L1	L2	L3	Total (k)
Branch - ref	Branch Id	8	1,000	1	2	75%	14	1	0	30
Customer	Driver Id	8	40,000	1	2	75%	547	2	1	1,100
	Licence Number	12	40,000	1	2	75%	656	2	1	1,318
	Customer Name	30	32,000	1.2	2	75%	936	3	1	1,880
Rental	Rental Id	10	260,000	1	2	75%	3,908	11	1	7,840
	Driver Id	8	40,000	6.5	2	75%	1,148	4	1	2,306
	Start Date	6	1,300	200	2	75%	723	2	1	1,452
	Car Group	2	5	30,000	2	75%	410	2	1	826
	Model id	8	15	4,000	2	75%	165	1	0	332
Booking	Booking Id	14	270,000	1	2	75%	4,796	14	1	9,622
	Branch (to)	10	40	400	2	75%	45	1	0	92
	Branch (from)	10	40	400	2	75%	45	1	0	92
	Start Date	6	1,000	200	2	75%	557	2	1	1,120
	End Date	6	1,000	200	2	75%	557	2	1	1,120
Car	Registration No	10	1,600	1	2	75%	25	1	0	52
	Stock Id	14	75	36	2	75%	9	1	0	20
	Delivery Id	20	150	2	2	75%	4	1	0	10
Paid Rental	Driver Id/Year	12	24,000	10	2	75%	984	3	1	1,976
										31,188

Figure 3-15 Spreadsheet of index sizing

The size of the indexes is usually not of major concern. What is important is the number of levels (indicated in the L1, L2, L3 columns in the spreadsheet) for frequently used indexes. Often, reducing the number of index levels (by, for example, increasing index block size) can have a significant effect on performance. See Optimising the Database Design, below.

3.6.5 *Optimising the Database Design*

The database designer/database administrator needs to apply optimisation techniques to the Database Design in a controlled way in order to meet pre-set performance objectives.

There are two principles used to moderate the optimisation process:

- Optimise only in order to achieve pre-set performance objectives. Optimisation helps to save space (in terms of data storage) and/or time (in terms of processing speed).

- Preserve the Logical Model within the system. The closer the implemented system is to the Logical Model, the easier it will be to understand and maintain.

The product-specific Database Design cannot be guaranteed to meet the performance objectives for the system, even though that design has been pre-optimised by application of heuristics (rules-of-thumb), such as the least dependent occurrence rule.

Set Storage and Timing constraints

Storage and Timing constraints can be derived from the requirements in the Requirements Catalogue, particularly the non-functional requirements.

Estimate storage requirements

Storage estimates are described above.

Restructure design to fit storage constraints

Storage constraints usually have only a minor impact on the final design. In EU-Rent, the space needed for data and indexes at each branch server is less that 250 Mbytes. Even quadrupling this to allow for work space, logging, software etc., would still require fairly modest cost.

Estimate resource times of major functions

The high-resource consuming functions are identified in Physical Process Design, and provided (preferably on the left-hand side of timing spreadsheets). They are almost always the ones that hit or create the entities with the most number of occurrences – usually the entities near the bottom of the Logical Data Model.

Rental Reservation								
Update/Enquiry	C	Entity	Aspect/sub-type	Access	Number	Index	Levels	Disk
Customer Details		Customer	Head Office	Read	0.04	Driver Id	3	0.12
		Annual Benefit	benefits	Read	0.12		2	
		Payment by Benefit		Read	0.48		2	
Customer Details		Customer	Head Office	Read	0.30	Driver Id	3	0.9
		Comment		Read	1.20		3	
Reservation		Rental	supertype	Create	1.00	Rental Id	3	8
		Paid Rental	free/paid	Create	1.00			
		Free Rental	benefits	Create	0.04			
		Annual Benefit	benefits	Modify	0.04			
Customer Rental	Ö	Customer	Head Office	Create	0.15	Driver Id	3	0.75
				Modify	0.85	Driver Id	3	3.4
Rental Start	Ö	Rental	direction	Create	1.00			
		Branch (prov)		Modify	1.00	Branch Id	3	4
		Branch (dest)		Modify	0.10	Branch Id	3	0.4
								17.57

Figure 3-16 Revised sizing spreadsheet

The sizing spreadsheet will give an estimate for the disk accesses required on the function. Note that it is assumed that for a frequently used index the top-level is assumed to be in memory, i.e., that for indexed access to a table with three levels of index, two index reads are needed, followed by one data read.

Identify problem areas

The data sizes and throughput requirements (<1500 rentals per server per week) mean that there are no significant performance issues for EU-Rent.

Exploit mechanisms for improving performance

There are some obvious areas for general performance improvement in the use of reference data. Branch service aspect and Depot can be merged into a 1-block table that can be held in RAM. Currently this can be done by realising a joined view and declaring it to be resident.

Similarly, manufacturer, group and model data can be merged into a single page that can be locked.

Reducing index levels from three to two reduces disk time for access from three reads to two. There are two ways of reducing index space:

- increase the block size; but this increases the amount of buffer space needed, increases swapping and weakens the assumption that top-level index blocks will usually be in RAM.

- reduce the index scope, e.g., by excluding history. This could be done by holding duplicates of columns used for indexes, when historical data is not required. For example, the index on Rental by start date is used to select Rentals for allocation of cars. If the Start Date column were duplicated, one for the historical value and one for indexing, the 'index' column could be set to NULL after allocation of a car. The index would have fewer targets and come down from three levels to two.

3.7   Relationship to other techniques

3.7.1 Logical Data Modelling (covered in the Data Modelling volume)

The Required System Logical Data Model and Data Catalogue are major inputs to Database Design. It is necessary to ensure that all volumes and entry points are documented on the Logical Data Model.

3.7.2 Requirements Definition (covered in The Business Context volume)

All non-functional requirements are potentially useful in the optimisation of the Database Design.

3.7.3 Function Definition (covered in the User Centred Design volume and the Function Modelling volume)

Optimisation is directed towards the performance of critical functions. The functions define the grouping of invocations of the event and enquiry processes (specified in Conceptual Process Modelling) which will be used for the detail of performance estimates. Service level requirements for critical functions will be useful as an input to optimisation.

Also, volumes of critical functions will be required.

3.7.4 Conceptual Process Modelling (covered in the Behaviour and Process Modelling volume)

Any Conceptual Process Modelling product which is related to one of the critical functions to be used in the optimisation of the Database Design may be useful as an input.

3.7.5 Technical System Options (covered in the SSADM Foundation volume)

The Technical System Architecture may give useful information to the designers.

4   PHYSICAL PROCESS DESIGN

Physical Process Design deals with the conversion of the products of logical design into physical program specifications for the chosen physical environment.

The technique guides designers in the approach to specifying a system's physical processes, from Logical Design, taking into account information about the selected physical processing system they are working with.

Physical Process Design covers a defined but generic range of design aspects and to a limited depth.

It is important in Physical Process Design to ensure that the work that has been expended on developing the logical design products is not wasted.

It should be noted that this chapter deals solely with the definition of physical process specifications. Screen, Interface and Window design is covered by the *User Centred Design* volume in this series and Database Design is covered in chapter 3 of this volume.

4.1   Physical Process Design and the System Development Template

The approach to Physical Process Design is based upon the three areas within Specification in the System Development Template. Two of these three areas have both logical and physical components as shown in Figure 4-1 (the physical areas are indicated by shading). Internal Design has physical components only.

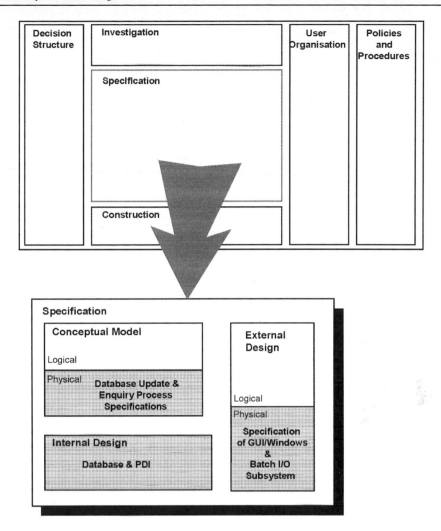

Figure 4-1 Physical Design in the System Development Template

In addition, the Function Component Implementation Map (FCIM) covers all three areas of Specification.

There is input and interaction with a number of different areas of the System Development Template as shown in Figure 4-2. The Requirements Catalogue provides much of the information about what is needed in the new system. Policies and Procedures will provide guidance and will impose constraints on what is done. The Technical System Architecture provides the basic technical architecture for the new system.

User procedures within the organisation will act as constraints on what is developed or will be devised as part of Physical Process Design.

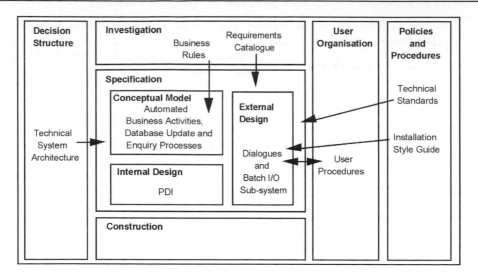

Figure 4-2 Interaction with other areas of the System Development Template

4.2   Inputs to Physical Process Design

The Technical System Architecture (TSA) will be a major input to the approach devised for Physical Process Design. The Technical System Architecture defines the various components of the new system and the technologies used for their implementation. The Technical System Architecture is produced as a product of Technical System Options which is described in *SSADM Foundation* in this series.

Another major input to Physical Process Design will come from within the Policies and Procedures of the organisation. These will provide the following:

- **Processing System Classification**. This will identify the features of the implementation technology that can be used. The precise features will depend upon the technology chosen but may include the types of tools that are available, mix of procedural and non-procedural languages, database processing and dialogue features;

- **Application Development Standards**. These standards will define criteria for deciding on the implementation technology for different components of functions, how to use the features of the implementation technology, how to undertake Physical Process Design and the standards for program specification. Many organisations will already have standards which can be used and adapted by specific projects. Where no standards exist, these will need to be developed before Physical Process Design is initiated.

The major input from within the logical design products will be the Function Definitions together with associated Conceptual Process Modelling products. A combination of these will provide very detailed information for the specification of physical processes. The aim within Physical Process Design should be to transform the logical design products into their physical equivalents rather than copying their content across to program specifications or developing program specifications from scratch with little direct reference to the logical design products. This transformation should, ideally, be supported by sophisticated facilities of the CASE tools being used on the project.

4.3   Physical Process Design Products

There may be many products developed as part of Physical Process Design depending upon local standards and policies. The following products should be considered for inclusion in the Physical Process Design:

- Function Component Implementation Map;
- Process Data Interface;
- Program Specifications.

4.3.1 The Function Component Implementation Map (FCIM)

The Function Component Implementation Map provides the overall structure of Physical Process Design. It defines:

- how logical specification components are grouped to define the content of physical components;
- how physical components fit together, including where components are reused.

The Function Component Implementation Map is supported by specifications for procedural fragments (the non-procedural fragments will generally be described using the language of the implementation environment itself).

The representation of the Function Component Implementation Map will vary from project to project, depending on the repository or dictionary facilities available. Possibilities include:

- if a single repository is used for logical and physical components, a set of logical-physical associations in the repository;
- if separate repositories are used for logical and physical components, a separate product maintaining logical-physical cross-references; for example, a diagram, a table, a small database.

The contents of a Function Component Implementation Map are described further in the section below, 'Create Function Component Implementation Map'.

4.3.2 The Process Data Interface

The Process Data Interface is a layer of software that hides the physical database from the database update and enquiry processes in the conceptual model. The database processes can then be written as if for the Logical Data Model.

At its simplest, the Process Data Interface might just be views of base tables and SQL calls to access them, embedded in database processes written in a host language such as COBOL or C.

In practice, it may not be possible to insulate all the processing from the database structure. Some processes may reflect the Database Design rather than the Logical Data Model, for reasons of performance or to take advantage of facilities provided by implementation tools for ease of programming or testing.

Some conceptual processes may have to be restructured to obtain performance from the database (typical cases include doing batch updates in two passes with the input sorted in different sequences, or postponing full updates for transactions input during peak hours).

4.3.3 Program specifications

Program generation from non-procedural code

The analyst may use non-procedural languages supplied with the physical environment to define the physical format of input and output data, and intermediate files. In some cases the analyst will also define database access paths in this way.

For some logical processes, the analyst will be able to generate the physical programs entirely from such a non-procedural specification. Where this is done, no further coding is needed after Physical Design.

Where programs cannot be so generated, the designer produces program specifications. There is no recommended standard for program specifications as this will be defined by local policies and procedures.

JSP-style program specification

For some procedural elements of the system the designer may use the principles of program design which underlie both the Structured Design Method (SDM) and Jackson Structured Programming (JSP).

The designer can use these principles to divide a function into distinct processes, and specify the input and output data structures of each process. In the case of database processes, the Conceptual Process Modelling products already include operations and conditions allocated to a processing structure. The next activity after Physical Design will be program coding from this design.

Constrained English and forms specification

For other procedural elements of the system or where a tool especially facilitates this approach, the designer may use a fragment or program specification. The language used may include structured English specification languages. The next activity after Physical Design will be program coding from this design.

Conventional program specification

For other procedural elements of the system, the designer may use a conventional program specification. The next activity after Physical Design will be design and coding of these procedural elements.

4.4   Procedure for Physical Process Design

Physical Process Design is undertaken in a number of steps:

- Prepare for Physical Design;
- Create Function Component Implementation Map;
- Complete Function Specification;
- Consolidate Process Data Interface.

This is only a suggested set of steps which may be modified as part of customisation. The activities covered by these steps are described in the following paragraphs. They should be modified to conform with local policies and procedures for undertaking Physical Process Design.

4.4.1 Prepare for Physical Process Design

This step is concerned with understanding the nature of the physical environment with regard to processing elements and planning the way forward for Physical Design.

The preparation for Physical Design consists of obtaining the required inputs to Physical Process Specification.

It is important to obtain all the knowledge required to design the physical processes. This will normally be achieved by bringing in experts in the physical environment or attending appropriate training courses.

In particular, if a Server based architecture is used, the Technical System Architecture can be used to clarify the style of the Client/Server implementation tools to be used. For example, with a 'Three-tier' approach, separate tools may exist for producing code fragments (and interchange/messaging specifications) on all three infrastructure components (client interface, application server, data server).

The logical design products that are used in Physical Process Specification are:

- the Requirements Catalogue;

- the Technical System Architecture developed to describe the selected Technical System Option;

- Conceptual Process Modelling products (Enquiry Access Paths and Effect Correspondence Diagrams or Enquiry Process Models and Update Process Models);

- User Interface Design products (Windows Navigation Model, Window Specifications and Help System Specifications);

- Function Definitions;

- Required System Logical Data Model.

In addition, the following standards should be obtained from local policies and procedures (or developed if they are not available):

- Application Style Guide;

- Application Naming Standards;

- Physical Design Strategy.

4.4.2 Create Function Component Implementation Map

The Function Component Implementation Map is:

- a mapping of logical specification components to the physical components to be developed;

- a specification of how physical components fit together, including where components are reused.

In creating the Function Component Implementation Map the designer must work at two different levels:

- looking for reusable processing across all functions;

- adding further detail to functions, specifying Function Component Implementation Map elements as fully as possible.

Reusable processing

It is clearly desirable that systems should be built in a modular fashion, reusing the code from physical fragments wherever it is effective to do so. All the logical design products should be examined to ascertain where common elements are present which can then have the processing defined once and then reused as necessary subject to commonality of implementation vehicle.

Adding further detail to functions

The following activities are applied to each function:

- define success units;

- specify syntax error handling;

- specify controls and control errors.

Each activity is described below.

Define success units

A success unit is the presentation of data to the program and the completion of all changes in each affected entity. A success unit can be defined as 'the smallest unit of consistent change to the system as a whole'.

The basic success unit is the event. However, it may be considered beneficial to group events into a larger success unit. For example, in the EU-Rent system, the event Walk-in Rental might have been modelled as three events with smaller scope:

- Creation of Rental;

- Rental Booking (assignment of Car to Rental);

- Car Pick-up.

These smaller events would succeed or fail as a single database transaction.

There are two issues that need to be considered regarding success units in enquiries. These issues are concerned with maintaining a consistent system state and with how data is locked:

- a pre-event enquiry should be part of the event's success unit;

- it may be important to maintain consistency during enquiries – all the data needed will have to be write-locked at the start of the enquiry. This may cause performance problems for updates that need records locked by long retrievals.

Specify syntax error handling

A syntactic error is an error condition detected in the input data. There are two reasons to postpone the specification of syntactic errors until now:

- it enables the designer to suppress less essential detail from the data definitions during earlier parts of the development project;

- syntactic errors are most conveniently specified in the manner prescribed by the physical environment.

There are two places to specify syntactic errors in a non-procedural language. The first is with a data item in the physical database specification (or meta-database), for example:

data item   :   age

error condition   :   not in range 0–150

error message   :   invalid age.

The second is with a data item in the physical input data specification, such as a screen definition. Errors which are unique to a specific function must be specified in this way.

It is generally better if error messages should be stored in and retrieved from the database, rather than coded into the processes, so that they can be maintained without altering the programs, and reused by several processes.

Specify controls and control errors

The types of control that are generally specified during Physical Design are either access controls or control of data error. Access controls are usually applied through the use of passwords or other means of hardware or software enforcement. Data errors can be controlled through a number of different mechanisms including the following:

- through dedicated audit function;

- check totals of given data item (either automatic or hand crafted);

- associated error reporting may require reinput of data or abort the function.

4.4.3 Complete Function Specification

There are two requirements for completion of the processing specification:

- bridging between the User Interface Design and the database processes;

- automation of business activities.

Bridging between the User Interface Design and the database processes

The bridging between the User Interface Design products and database processes will, in the majority of cases, be a relatively straightforward process in that a function will often require a single window. It is unlikely that any further specification will be needed for this type of function. However, it is possible that the data input and output through the User Interface Design products does not match the event and enquiry data specified in Effect Correspondence Diagrams and Enquiry Access Paths. In this case, some form of transformation process will be required. This transformation may involve:

- decomposing input data into multiple event/enquiry triggers, possibly including selections and iterations of events and enquiries;

- reference data look-ups (pre-event enquiries that are not made visible to the dialogue) and local calculation.

The function may have to consolidate event and enquiry response data for presentation to the user. This may involve:

- collating responses from several events/enquiries;

- sorting, suppressing duplicates;

- calculation of summary data.

Automation of business activities

Each business activity that is to be automated will contain rules that have to be expressed in a form that can be implemented. There are two broad options for the implementation of business rules:

- a rule interpretation system, which operates on declarative statements of rules. The rules have to be expressible in the form required by the interpreter, typically in some version of predicate logic specifying pre- and post-conditions. Encoding the rules in the required syntax may require a specialist who will have to be provided with a rules component specification, analogous to a program specification;

- procedural implementation. The rules have to be stated unambiguously in a form that can be transformed into an algorithm.

In all cases, a decision has to be made on which components of the Client/Server architecture are to be used for implementing these activities.

4.4.4 Consolidate Process Data Interface

Using the physical environment the designer may be able to specify the Process Data Interface in a non-procedural language. Most modern DBMSs offer support for defining 'logical views' of the physical database. The specification of each logical view will comprise:

- the operation desired upon the Logical Data Model;

- the operations necessary upon the physical database;

- non-procedural specification of the physical access path.

Otherwise, the Process Data Interface should be specified as a set of procedural modules.

The access requirements for function components which have been specified in the Function Component Implementation Map are matched against the Database Design (optimised) and mismatches identified. During the optimisation of the Database Design some of these will have been identified.

The new processing components formed are compared to detect duplication. Then the Process Data Interface elements should be fully documented in the Function Component Implementation Map showing the interactions which handle the mismatches between the logical and physical views of the accesses.

4.5   Relationship with other techniques

4.5.1 *Function Definition (covered in the* User Centred Design *volume and the* Function Modelling *volume)*

Function Definitions are a major input to Physical Process Specification. Functions are part of External Design. For many functions, the mapping from input to event/enquiry trigger is simple but for some there is a significant process, distinct from the dialogue, which is required to interpret dialogue input into event/enquiry input and transform event/enquiry output into dialogue output. During the creation of the Function Component Implementation Map, syntactic errors, which will be detected by the input processes, are specified and common processes identified.

4.5.2 *User Interface Design (covered in the* User Centred Design *volume)*

The products of User Interface Design (Window Navigation Model, Window Specifications and Help System Specifications) are examined to check that no gap exists between them and the physical process specifications

4.5.3 *Conceptual Process Modelling (covered in the* Behaviour and Conceptual Process Modelling *volume)*

The Effect Correspondence Diagrams, Enquiry Access Paths, Update Processes Models and Enquiry Process Models will provide the basis for the definition of database processing within the system. Operations and conditions from Conceptual Process Modelling products can be directly implemented in a non-procedural language. In addition, new physical processes may be required which implement business rules that are not embedded in event and enquiry processes.

4.5.4 *Database Design (covered in Chapter 3)*

New performance requirements identified in Database Design will form part of the Process Data Interface. These may take the form of sort routines in physical run units. Such processes may be triggered and reported back by on-line processes.

5   PRODUCT DESCRIPTIONS FOR PHYSICAL DESIGN

5.1   Application Development Standards

Purpose

To define the appropriate standards to be used throughout the application design, construction and testing stages. This product may be made available from within other parts of the organisation.

Composition

- Application Naming Standards
- Application Style Guide
- Physical Design Strategy
- Physical Environment Classification

Position in System Development Template

Policies and Procedures.

Quality Criteria:

Are all necessary standards set?

External Dependencies

1   Existence of the relevant installation standards documents.

2   Availability of information concerning the (physical) implementation and development environments.

5.2   Function Component Implementation Map (FCIM)

Purpose

To classify and specify the implementation fragments needed to meet the processing requirements for all function components of the Function Definitions. The classification is in terms of the object types supported by the physical environment.

The document has four sub-goals, namely:

- to eliminate duplicate components and fragments;
- to reuse common components and fragments;
- to specify the implementation route to be followed;
- to package components into success units.

The FCIM documentation set should be implemented to local standards.

Suitability

The FCIM is an important element of Physical Design and is particularly suitable where there is significant reuse of update, enquiry and user interface components across functions.

The FCIM is suitable where:

- complexity of functions is high;
- the number of replications of the computer system is high;
- the complexity of the target technology is high;
- the importance of technical change is high.

Composition

Cross-reference of function components and fragments showing uses of and use by relationships.

Cross-reference of function components and fragments showing form of implementation (tool facility used, procedural and non-procedural specification and languages)

Detailed processing specifications each including:

- the purpose of the procedure;
- its relationship with other procedures;

- inputs and outputs;
- summary of operation which may be classified using one or more of the following:
    - non-procedural code;
    - other forms of procedural specification including constrained natural language and formal notations such as Z;
    - for some programs or run units it will be necessary to add all or some of the following:
        - structure of the job in terms of constituent programs; hardware requirements; files (media; sort orders; names; volumes and volatility); file and record layouts not previously defined; references to defined layouts; operations required to drive output from input; controls and restarts; special requirements (eg library routines and security requirements)
        - manual procedures, including detail covering the purpose of the procedure, position in sub-system and relationship to other procedures and programs, inputs and outputs; human and material resource requirements; implications of operations and management policies; timing; development estimate
    - Jackson structure diagrams and supporting documentation.

Position in System Development Template

Specification

Quality Criteria:

For each component:

1   Is the implementation technique appropriate?

2   Is the nature of each component or fragment properly described in terms of purpose, inputs, outputs, action (and variations) and usage?

3   Are the non-procedurally encoded specifications validated using the tools of the physical environment (i.e., do they compile)?

4   Has each specification (especially the procedural ones) been subjected to a structured walk-through?

5   Have all walk-through results been documented?

6   Are all forms of clash resolved?

7   Do run schedules have valid internal dependencies?

8   Will run units meet required service levels?

For the set:

9   Is every function definition component implementation shown on the map?

10   Is every function component cross-referenced to a processing fragment?

11   Are the cross-references fully documented (preferably using the facilities of the physical environment)?

External Dependencies

1   Object types supported in the physical environment.

2   Facilities for documentation and cross-referencing in the physical environment.

3   Flexibility of physical environment facilities.

5.3   Database Design

Purpose

To produce an implementation specific data design that ensures that the system meets performance objectives expressed in terms of machine space and levels of service and which can used to implement the Data Dictionary for the system.

The performance of the product specific Database Design is evaluated and the design modified to ensure that it meets the objectives defined by the users.

Suitability

Database Design is suitable wherever it is necessary to implement a Logical Data Model onto a physical database and where tuning of this Database Design is needed to meet performance objectives.

Composition

This is dependent on the implementation vehicle and shows how the Required System LDM is to be implemented in the physical system. The documentation may include any or all of the following:

- Database Design (first-cut);

- Database Design (optimised);

- Space estimation form(s) (to be designed for the characteristics of a particular DBMS);

- Timing estimating form(s) (to be designed for the characteristics of a particular DBMS).

Note: for the space estimation, the following sample data should be collected and manipulated in a spreadsheet:

- block/page type;

- block/page size (kbytes);

- block/page working capacity (e.g., kbytes at 60%);

- record type (entity id for row);

- primary owner;

- number of record instances per hierarchy;

- record data size in bytes;

- record storage overhead;

- relationship overheads;

- pointer to each master;

- pointer to each detail;

- total space per record (bytes);

- cumulative space for hierarchy;

- cumulative space in block;

- data total;

- block header;

- block total.

Note: for the timing estimation, the following sample data should be collected and manipulated in a spreadsheet.

- Rows:

    - Read direct via index;

    - Read direct via pointer chain;

    - Read next in database;

    - Update in place;

    - Update in place/modify pointer chain;

    - Create;

    - Delete.

- Columns:

    - Average read time (including rotational delay and latency);

    - Average write time (including rotational delay, latency and any read after write check);

    - Load time for blocks into memory;

    - Average time for DBMS software to interpret and execute call;

    - Average time for TPMS to queue/de-queue physical I/O calls;

    - Average time for operating system to schedule operations.

Position in System Development Template

Specification.

Quality Criteria:

1.   Is the data design implementable in the chosen physical environment?

2.   Does the design meet performance objectives?

3.   Will the resultant DBMS operate efficiently in the available disc and memory space?

4.   Are all Logical Data Model entities and relationships implemented in the physical DBMS?

5.   Are batching elements (transient data stores) incorporated?

6.   Can the DBMS support all the physical processing to the required level of service?

7.   Is the data design fully documented?

8.   Is the optimised Database Design consistent with the product specific data design?

External Dependencies

1.   Availability of suitable product information to establish the validity (or not) of the design.

2.   Appropriateness of chosen product to priority requirements.

3.   Availability of optimisation expertise.

4.   Availability of accurate timing factor information.

5.4   Physical Process Specification

Purpose

To package all the specifications for the system processing to enable construction, testing and commissioning of the proposed system to be completed.

To provide a documentation base on which future maintenance, enhancement, end-user support (such as information centre services), error handling and help desk activities can draw. The level of detail required, and the format of the specifications, is dependent on the target environment and installation standards.

Composition

- Data Catalogue – probably implemented in a data dictionary.
- Function Component Implementation Map.
- Function Definition (with additional data optimisation and PDI requirements).
- Requirements Catalogue (noting any design trade-offs or compromises made in the course of Physical Design).
- Required System Logical Data Model.

Position in System Development Template

Specification.

Quality Criteria:

1   Are all components complete and consistent?

2   Does all the documentation conform to the constraints of the physical environment, the Requirements Catalogue and the Technical System Architecture?

External Dependencies

1   Existence of installation standards for producing these facilities.

2   Availability of design and language expertise.

5.5   Process Data Interface (PDI)

Purpose

To document the interface between the implemented Database Design and all the components of the Physical Process Specification. This interface should make the database implemented appear like the Required System Logical Data Model to the processing components. The aim of this is to ease understandability and maintenance. It will also minimise the impact of change.

It allows the designer to implement the logical update and enquiry processes as physical programs, independently of the physical database structure.

Suitability

The PDI is suitable where portability and flexibility of the proposed system are of significant importance and where the logical process models are to be protected from changes made to the Database Design. The PDI is of particular importance in Client Server type development.

Composition

- Fragment specification for DBMS accesses (from Function Component Implementation Map).

- Fragment specification for declarative syntax and control utilities (from Function Component Implementation Map).

Position in System Development Template

Specification – Internal Design.

Quality Criteria:

1   Are all necessary requirements documented?

2   Are all update data views supported?

3   Are all enquiry data views supported?

4   Are all physical DBMS navigation paths explicitly cross-referenced to the Required System LDM?

5   Are all processing interfaces defined?

6   Are installation standards followed with regard to data administration facilities?

7   Do the DBMS access fragments meet performance requirements?

External Dependencies

1   Level of knowledge of the characteristics and functionality of the implementation language.

2   Extent to which the Database Design is a one-to-one mapping with the Required System Logical Data Model.

ANNEXE A – DESCRIPTION OF SYSTEM DEVELOPMENT TEMPLATE

The System Development Template (SDT) provides a common structure for the overall system development process. This template is used extensively in the definition of SSADM.

The System Development Template divides the development process into a number of distinct areas of concern, as shown in the diagram below.

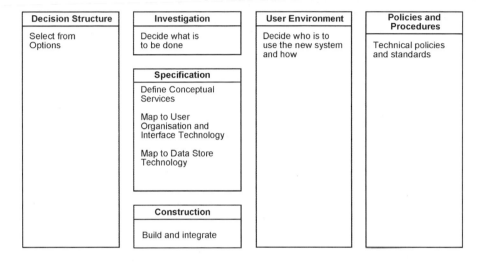

Figure A-1 System Development Template general view

The 3-schema specification architecture (which covers the Specification area) concentrates on those products that will ultimately lead, sometimes via other products, into elements of software. The SDT takes a broader view and divides the system development process into activity areas onto which all the development products may be mapped.

ANNEXE B – DESCRIPTION OF EU-RENT CASE STUDY

EU-Rent is a car rental company owned by EU-Corporation. It is one of three businesses – the other two being hotels and an airline – that each have their own business and IT systems, but share their customer base. Many of the car rental customers also fly with EU-Fly and stay at EU-Stay hotels.

EU-Rent business

EU-Rent has 1000 branches in towns all over Europe. At each branch cars, classified by car group, are available for rental. Each branch has a manager and booking clerks who handle rentals.

Rentals

Most rentals are by advance reservation; the rental period and the car group are specified at the time of reservation. EU-Rent will also accept immediate ('walk-in') rentals, if cars are available.

At the end of each day cars are assigned to reservations for the following day. If more cars have been requested than are available in a group at a branch, the branch manager may ask other branches if they have cars they can transfer to him/her.

Returns

Cars rented from one branch of EU-Rent may be returned to any other branch. The renting branch must ensure that the car has been returned to some branch at the end of the rental period. If a car is returned to a branch other than the one that rented it, ownership of the car is assigned to the new branch.

Servicing

EU-Rent also has service depots, each serving several branches. Cars may be booked for maintenance at any time provided that the service depot has capacity on the day in question.

For simplicity, only one booking per car per day is allowed. A rental or service may cover several days.

Customers

A customer can have several reservations but only one car rented at a time. EU-Rent keeps records of customers, their rentals and bad experiences such as late return, problems with payment and damage to cars. This information is used to decide whether to approve a rental.

Current IT system

Each branch and service depot has a local IT system based on PCs and a file server. The equipment is obsolete and limited in capacity (especially RAM). Hardware failures – screens, disk drives and power supplies – are increasingly frequent. There is currently no use of the Internet either for customer to business communication or for business to business communication.

Application maintainability

The application programs have been maintained over several years. Small RAM in the PCs has necessitated intricate, complex programs which makes amendments progressively more difficult and expensive.

Informal communication

Each location operates almost independently of others. Communication between locations is mainly by phone and fax and co-ordination is very variable. Sometimes, when a car is dropped off at a branch different from the pick-up branch, the drop-off branch will not inform the pick-up branch.

Branch managers tend to co-operate in small groups and not to look for 'spare' cars outside those groups. EU-Rent management feels that some capacity is wasted, but does not have reliable estimates of how much.

Scheduling of service bookings in branch and service depot files is co-ordinated by faxes between branch and depot. Sometimes service bookings are not recorded in the branch files, and cars booked for servicing are rented. Service depots sometimes do not get to know that a car has been transferred to a branch served by other depots until another depot requests the car's service history.

Customer blacklist

A copy of the customer blacklist is held at every branch. It should be updated every week from head office, but the logistics of updating the list with input from 1000 sources and sending out 1000 disks every week are beyond head office's capability. Updates are in fact sent out about every four weeks.

E-Commerce

There is no current use of e-commerce with customers having to phone or fax the individual offices to book cars for rental. This is causing problems in that some competitors have introduced facilities that enable customers to book and monitor their bookings over the Internet and it is thought that this is resulting in a loss of custom.

IT system replacement

EU-Rent management has decided that a new IT system is needed. It is expected whilst the basic operational activity is not expected to change significantly – locations and volume of rentals – it is expected that a number of 'online' systems (e.g. ordering of cars) will be implemented not necessarily as part of the initial role out but shortly thereafter. The new system is justified on three grounds:

- the current system cannot be kept going much longer;

- the perceived need to introduce some online system that can be accessed directly by customers over the Internet;

- better management of numbers of cars at branches and better co-ordination between branches is expected to increase utilisation of cars slightly – the same volume of business should be supportable with fewer cars. Each car ties up about 8,000 Euros in capital and loses about 3,000 Euros in depreciation, so significant savings are possible from small reductions in numbers of cars needed.

Corporate data

After the current IT system has been replaced, EU-Rent management wants to explore possibilities for sharing customer data across the car rental, hotel and airline systems. Even if customers are not stored in a single shared database, it makes sense for all three business areas to have consistent customer information on current address, telephone number, credit rating, etc.

It will be useful to know in each system when there are problems with a customer in other systems. And it may be possible to run promotions in one system, based on what EU-Corporation knows from the other systems about customers.

Future requirements

A customer loyalty incentive scheme is also under consideration. The requirement is not yet precisely defined but the scheme will be comparable with those offered by EU-Rent's competitors.

Members of the scheme will accumulate credit points with each car rental. They will exchange points for 'free' rentals. Only the base rental price will be payable by points; extra charges such as insurance and fuel will be paid for by cash or credit card. When this is introduced it is expected that customers will wish to be able to check (either by the use of a call-centre or directly over the Internet) the current state of their credit points.

Rationale for EU-Rent

The business of EU-Rent is car rentals, but this is largely irrelevant; it merely provides an easily understood context for examples. The business issues and user requirements in EU-Rent could be easily mapped to other systems. They include:

- a requirement to deliver a range of services (rental of cars of different quality and price) at many locations (rental branches), with different volumes of business and patterns of demand;

- customers who may use more than one location, but whose business with the whole organisation should be tracked;

- strong general policies set centrally (car models that may be used, rental tariffs, procedures for dealing with customers), but significant flexibility and authority for local managers (number of cars owned by branch, authority to over-ride published tariff to beat competitors' prices);

- a requirement for customers to be able to directly access aspects of the system;

- performance targets for local managers;

- a requirement for capacity planning and resource replenishment (disposal and purchase of cars, moving of cars between branches); possibilities for this to be managed locally, regionally or centrally;

- locally-managed sharing or swapping of resources or customers between branches to meet short-term unforeseen demand;

- an internal support structure (the maintenance depots) needed to maintain the resources and ensure that the product delivered to customers is of adequate quality;

- a customer base that is shared with other, separate systems (EU-Stay hotels and EU-Fly airline), and possibilities of communicating or co-ordinating with these systems.

Many of these characteristics are common to other types of business; for example, health care, vocational training, social security, policing, retail chain stores, branch banking.

ANNEXE C - GLOSSARY OF TERMS

3-Schema Specification Architecture

The Three-schema Specification Architecture has been introduced into the SSADM rationale as means of understanding the method's structure, in particular the distinction between the modelling of business rules, the user interface and the physical implementation of data management. This helps maintain a level of independence between the logical business requirements and the system implementation strategy, thus increasing the flexibility and robustness of the system design.

The Three-schema Specification Architecture divides the system design into three areas or 'views'.

- Conceptual Model;
- Internal Design;
- External Design.

Application Development Standards

Defines the standards which apply to the physical design and development activities, for this project/application.

Application Naming Standards

Defines the naming conventions for all aspects of the application under development, with particular emphasis being placed on constraints imposed by the (physical) implementation environment.

Application Style Guide

Should be regarded as a set of standards, covering the user interface, to be followed within a particular application development. This document is based on the Installation Style Guide and tailored to the specific needs of a particular project.

Conceptual Model

The Conceptual Model comprises the essential business rules and knowledge. It is a system model which is independent of the user interface and hence is portable between different implementation environments. It is possible to believe, in some respects, that there is a 'right' answer to Conceptual Model design. SSADM expresses the Conceptual Model as a Logical Data Model and models of the interaction between entities and events/enquiries.

Database Design

Technique

Takes the Required System Logical Data Model and translates it into a product-specific database design within the chosen technical environment with consideration having been given to performance and space constraints.

Product

The definition for the physical database which is to be implemented. The design is developed in two steps; the first produces a 'first-cut' design based on applying rules about the DBMS to the Requires System Logical Data Model; the second is a design optimised for performance reasons.

Database Management System (DBMS)

The mechanism for managing data held within a computerised system. Conceptually data is held within one file regardless of how the content is physically organised.

DBMS Data Storage Classification

For analysing and recording data storage and retrieval mechanisms of DBMS or file handler.

DBMS Performance Classification

Records the factors which impact on the performance of a DBMS or file handler.

function

A user-defined packaging of events and enquiries and the processing they trigger that will be accessed from the External Design. Functions can be categorised as enquiry/update, off-line/on-line, user-initiated/system initiated.

Function Component Implementation Map (FCIM)

A classification and specification of all implementation fragments for all function components defined in the Function Definitions to meet the processing requirements.

Function Definition

The product of the Function Definition technique is a group products called the Function Definition. This is composed of the following products:

- Function Description;
- I/O Structure.

Function Description

The Function Description contains some descriptive text and a large number of cross-references to other products. The precise format of the product will depend upon the documentation tools available to the project.

functional requirement

Functional requirements are those for particular features or facilities, describing 'what' the system should do. For example:

- updates;
- enquiries;
- reports/outputs;
- data (data items, entities, relationships);
- interactions with other systems.

installation development standards

Input to Physical Design. Documents the criteria which should be used during the development of all Information Systems within the organisation/installation. Note precise details of the contents of this Product are not given within this volume set.

Installation Style Guide

Is a set of standards for the development of all automated systems within an organisation. The guide contains standards about the nature, approach and style of the human factors aspects of computerised systems. The standards should be followed by all projects undertaken within an organisation. The Installation Style Guide can be elaborated to produce an Application Style Guide.

Internal Design

Part of the Three-schema Specification Architecture within the System Development Template. The Internal Design defines the physical database design and the process/data interface. There is a dependency on trade-offs, between such factors as timing, space utilisation and maintainability. It is a creative area where there is no 'right' answer. Heuristic approaches may be appropriate.

Logical Data Model

Provides an accurate model of the information requirements of all or part of an organisation. This serves as a basis for file and database design, but is independent of any specific implementation technique or product.

The Logical Data Model consists of a Logical Data Structure, Entity Descriptions and Relationship Descriptions. Associated descriptions of attribute/data items and domains are maintained in the Data Catalogue.

Logical Data Structure

A diagrammatic representation of the information needs of an organisation in the form of entities and the relationships between them.

The Logical Data Structure formalises the structure of information by depicting diagrammatically the different types of relationship in which entities can participate.

A Logical Data Structure consists of two basic components:

- entities;
- relationships.

non-functional requirement

A requirement which describes how, how well or to what level of quality a facility of the system should be provided. Examples include service level requirements, access restrictions, security, monitoring, audit and control, usability and constraints.

Physical Design Strategy

Documents all aspects relating to designing the physical implementation of the system.

Physical Environment Classification

Classifies the environment in which the application is to be implemented. Also describes the development environment and migration path where necessary.

Physical Environment Specification

Specifies the hardware and software products and services to be supplied, commissioned and made available for implementation. Generally this will be provided by the vendor.

Physical Process Specification

Packages all of the specifications for processing which are required in the proposed system. This is sometimes known as Program Specifications.

Process Data Interface

Documents how the Logical Data Model can be mapped onto the Physical Data Design, showing how it interfaces with the Physical Processing Specification. It allows the designer to implement the logical update and enquiry processes as physical programs, independently of the physical database structure.

Processing System Classification

Classifies the details of the processing environment which is to be used for implementation. Where appropriate, it also defines the development environment.

Required System Logical Data Model

Provides the detail of the proposed system information requirements. It is developed during the Requirements Specification and Logical System Specification Modules. It is compared with the results of Relational Data Analysis to produce a normalised model.

requirement

Describes a required feature of the proposed system. Requirements may be functional (describing what the system should do) or non-functional (describing how a facility should be provided, or how well, or to what level of quality). Documented as part of Requirements Definition in the Requirements Catalogue.

Requirements Catalogue

Is the central repository for information covering all identified requirements, both functional and non-functional. Each entry is textual and describes a required facility or feature of the proposed system.

success unit

Is a set of processing which must succeed or fail as a whole within the system. When a failure occurs the system is restored to the state it was in immediately before the 'success unit' began.

System Development Template

The System Development Template provides a common structure for the overall system development process.

It divides the process into a number of distinct areas of concern:

- Investigation;
- Specification;
- Construction;
- Decision Structure;
- User Organisation;
- Policies and Procedures.

The Specification area contains the Three-schema Specification Architecture which is made up of the areas Conceptual Model, Internal Design and External Design. The Three-schema Specification Architecture concentrates on those products that will ultimately lead, sometimes via other products, into elements of software. The System Development Template takes a broader view. It divides the system development process into activity areas onto which the development products may be mapped.

Technical System Architecture

Provides the specification of the technical environment which is produced once the Technical System Option has been selected. This detail is then passed on to physical design activities.

Technical System Options

The set of Technical System Options which has been developed so that the system development direction can be chosen.

Each option documents the functions to be incorporated and details implementation requirements. Each description is textual with some planning information. Functional elements are taken directly from the Requirements Specification

INDEX